Sounds and Shadows

Reading Practice

owl	out
cow	our
now	mouth
howl	pouch
brown	bound
power	ground
scowl	about

boy	oil
toy	boil
destroy	coin
annoy	voice
enjoy	spoil

At the bottom of each page of text, some multisyllable words are split up for the reader.

Contents

Vocabulary:

jet lag — extreme tiredness felt by a person after a long flight

growling — making a low throat sound, indicating hostility

streaming — flowing steadily

mock — fake in a teasing, joking way

loyal — faithful, constantly supportive

coward — a person lacking in the courage to deal with dangerous or unpleasant things

scowl — an angry or bad-tempered expression

pounced — sprang forward suddenly

toppled — overbalanced and fell to the ground

prowling — moving stealthily in search of prey

shuddered — shook uncontrollably

rotten — decayed or decomposed

Danny had set up a charity that collected plastic bottles from the beach and turned them into greenhouses. He showed Jack and Ash how to join the bottles together.

"It can take a thousand bottles to make a greenhouse," he said. "But it is a great way of using plastic from the sea."

green hous es   to geth er   thou sand

"Danny knows all there is to know about Bayma Island," said Gran. "He has often helped me with filming. He's going to take us into the forest to film the turtles."

film ing

Danny tipped oil into a pan and stirred in eggs and veg. He handed Jack back his necklace. "I was trying to work out how this had found its way onto the beach," he said with a grin. "Now, let's eat!"

Jack stretched. Jet lag had suddenly hit him. Gran patted his hand.

"Sleep now, Jack," she said. "We're all going into the forest tomorrow." Jack gazed around him with a puzzled frown. Were they going to sleep on the ground?

sudd en ly

Danny pointed into the forest. Jack was amazed to see a house in the trees.

"The beds are made of plastic bottles too!" yelled Danny.

"I hope the toilet is real," grinned Ash.

point ed   toi let

Chapter 2: A Bad Dream

Jack dropped into a deep sleep. He dreamt
he was being chased by a growling beast. He
woke up shaking.

"It was just a dream," he told himself. The sun
was streaming into the house. He was glad to
get up.

growl ing   stream ing

Gran was crouching next to a pot, boiling up tea. She handed round Grandpa's leftover cakes. Jack was still feeling shaky from his dream. He tucked his honey cake into his pocket.

crouch ing   left o ver

They all set off into the forest. There was so much to see. Ash tucked a pink flower into her hair. Jack gave a mock bow.

"The royal queen of the forest," he joked, "and I am your loyal servant."

flow er   loy al   serv ant

Chapter 3: Bee Careful!

When they got going again, they saw the track had split into three. Jack frowned. They'd been left behind. Where were Danny and Gran? "Danny!" he shouted loudly.

Ash pointed to the left. "I think they went this way. If we run, we'll catch them up."

go ing   loud ly

Jack tried to ring Gran as they ran.
"No joy. The phone won't work here," he
groaned. Suddenly, the track ran out.
"This can't be the way," said Ash. "Let's stop.
It's safer to stay in one place and wait until
they come back."

sa fer

Ash pointed out a cloud hanging over a tree. There was a loud buzzing noise. It made Jack think of Grandpa.

"Bees!" he told Ash. "We can eat the honey!" There were hundreds of bees.

"I think you've met your match with those bees," teased Ash.

buzz ing   hun dreds

11

"I'm not a coward," said Jack with a scowl.
"I'm going up!" He clambered up the tree.
The sound of the bees got louder. He kept his
mouth shut to keep the bees out.

cow ard   loud er

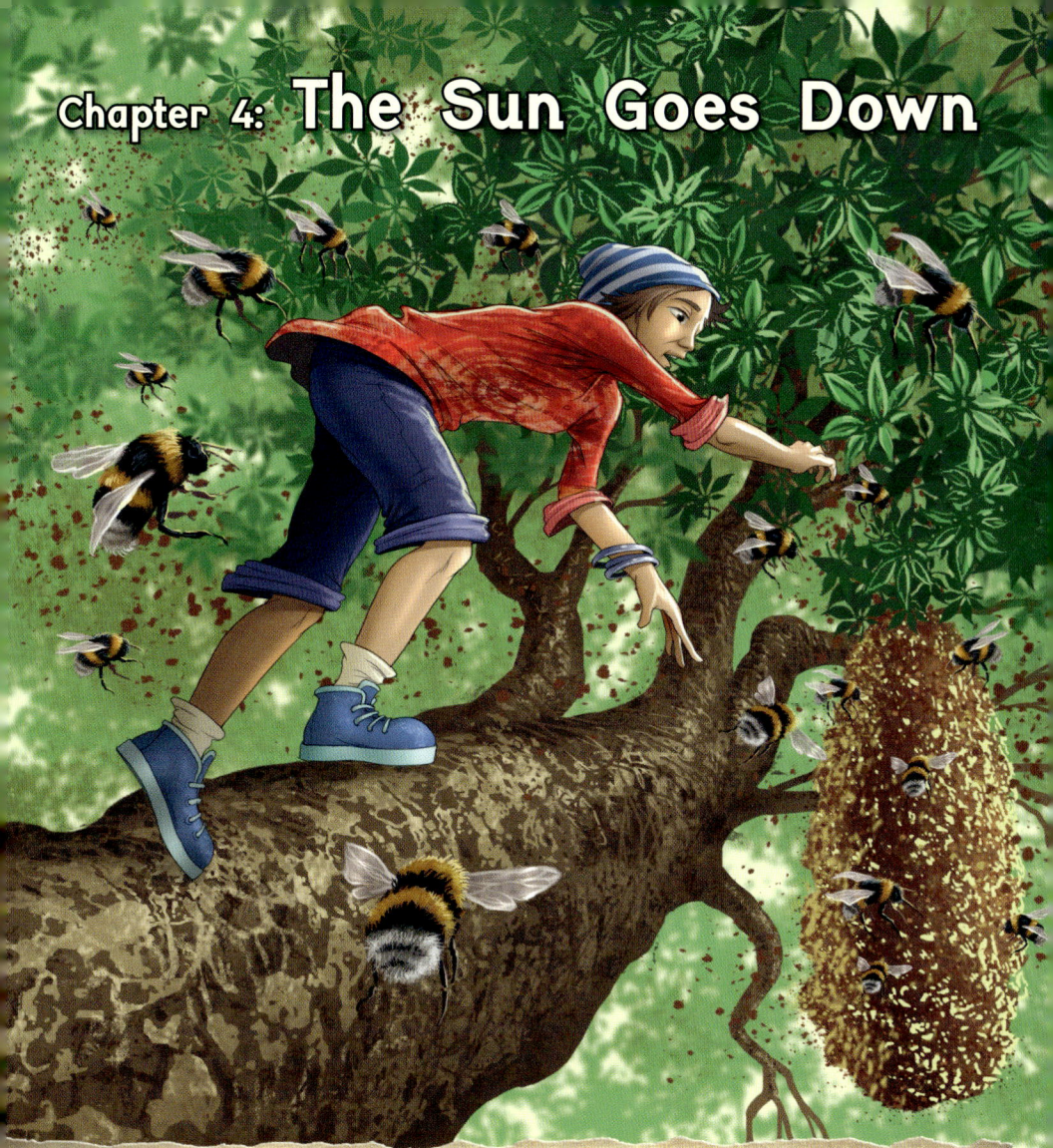

A crowd of angry bees surrounded him.
"I wish I'd let Grandpa teach me about bees,"
muttered Jack. He pounced on the honey. He
missed the honey and toppled out of the tree!

surr ound ed

Jack landed on the ground with a thud. Ouch!
A bundle dropped out of his pocket. The cake!
"Oh well," he told Ash. "We may not have the
honey, but at least we have honey cake! Let's
eat this, and think of a plan."

The sun was going down. Shadows filled the forest. Suddenly, Jack began to panic. He remembered the prowling beast in his dream and shuddered.

"We need a safe place to sleep," he told Ash.

re mem bered   shudd ered

Ash spotted an old, rotten boat hidden in the shrub. They dragged it out and turned it over. "We can sleep under it," said Jack. "Tomorrow we'll track down Gran and Danny."

rott en   to morr ow